FAMILY FR

Edited by Dar

GET A JOB
Paul Hurt

BATTLE LINES
Tony Coult

END OF THE ROAD
Kara May

STAND UP AND BE COUNTED
Tony Coult

ON THE PILL
Kara May

Published by arrangement with BBC Books,
a division of BBC Enterprises Ltd

Heinemann Educational Books

HEINEMANN EDUCATIONAL BOOKS LTD
22 Bedford Square, London WC1B 3HH

LONDON   EDINBURGH   MELBOURNE   AUCKLAND
SINGAPORE   KUALA LUMPUR   NEW DELHI
IBADAN   NAIROBI   JOHANNESBURG
PORTSMOUTH (NH)   KINGSTON

The scripts in this book were first broadcast by BBC School Radio in 1986, produced by Dan Garrett.

First published in 1988

ISBN 0 435 23000 X

Typeset by Latimer Trend & Company Ltd.
Printed and bound in Great Britain by
J. W. Arrowsmith Ltd, Bristol

CONTENTS

Foreword

Family Frictions is an excellent idea. Young people have always had so much to say about what goes on around them, and it is important that their thoughts, their ideals, fears and opinions are heard. And it's important for me too to know what's going on so that I can reflect those feelings in my programmes.

I saw all these plays when BBC School Radio took them on the road, and was very impressed by the discussions that followed. Open discussion is healthy, and stems bigotry and narrow-mindedness. Each play focuses on one particular issue and all the issues . . . jobs, the Youth Training Scheme, football violence, getting old, standing up for what you believe in and sexual relationships . . . are terribly important when you are about to leave the cosy environment of school or college and step into the big bad world on your own.

A few hundred young people saw these plays being recorded; thousands heard them broadcast, and now it's great news that they're being published so that many more thousands can have the opportunity to read them, act them and then get talking about really important issues.

They made me think. I hope you'll get as much out of them as I did.

Take care
love
Janice x

Janice Long

Introduction

The plays in this book began life when the editor and the three writers met to create a radio series called 'Teenage Plays'. Unusually for radio, the five plays were each to be rehearsed for several days, the actors were to learn their lines, and the recordings were to be made in front of a live audience. After each play, we planned to have a discussion between the audience and the actors, who would stay in character. This approach is often used by Theatre-in-Education teams. It's called 'hot-seating'.

The plays were performed in three separate venues, Alfreton School in Derbyshire, Robert Clack Comprehensive School in Dagenham, and the West End Drama Centre in Aldershot. Pop DJ Janice Long introduced them to mixed audiences of about seventy students and led the discussion afterwards.

The results were as lively as we had hoped, and the actors gave as good as they got. They challenged the views and opinions flung at them when things got heated and sometimes reached a surprising measure of agreement with their audience. One of the most eloquent contributions was from a young Dagenham student who affirmed her belief in 'saving herself for marriage' in the face of disbelief and disagreement from most of her companions.

You may possess recordings of the original BBC School Radio broadcasts. There are very minor differences between the published texts and the live performances – the kind of slight changes that actors make during rehearsal and in performance.

Dan Garrett

Introduction

The characters were first created by the following actors:

SANDY	Noreen Leighton
PETE	Lee Galpin
MR BARRETT	John Talbot
MRS BARRETT	Syd Ralph
GRANDAD	Lockwood West
RICHARD	Martin Barrass
CAROL, VANESSA	Theresa Boden
MRS CLAYTHORPE	Sandra Clark

GET A JOB!

CHARACTERS

SANDY

PETE

MR BARRETT

MRS BARRETT

SCENE *The Barretts' café in a small Yorkshire town.*

There is a counter to the back of the stage on which rests a large urn; beside this is a display case filled with sandwiches, tea-cakes, chocolate biscuits and the like; on top of the display case are several clean cups with saucers. In front of the counter is a table with three chairs resting upside down on its top. Although clean and tidy, the café is small and quite claustrophobic, and has seen better days.

It is early morning in the café and SANDY *is standing behind the counter stirring a cup of tea, listening to a cassette-player which is standing on the counter, playing a tape of Billy Bragg singing 'To Have and to Have Not'.*

Enter MR BARRETT, *Sandy's father, who switches the cassette-player off.*

SANDY: 'Ey-up! I was listening to that.

MR BARRETT: You'll make your ears badly listening to that rubbish ... Here, letter for you.

SANDY: For me?

MR BARRETT: Well, I think it's for you, it's got your name on the front. Unless your mother's been sending off for those free offers again.

SANDY: Well, what is it?

MR BARRETT: How the hell do I know? I haven't got X-ray vision you know ... Perhaps if you were to open it you'd find out.

(MR BARRETT *hands the letter to* SANDY.)

SANDY: Ta.

MR BARRETT: Have you filled the machines? Sandra?

SANDY: What? Oh, yeah ...

MR BARRETT: Coffee?

SANDY (*reading letter*): No, ta, I've got a cup of tea.

MR BARRETT: I'm not asking if you want a cup, I'm asking if you filled the Espresso.

SANDY: Hey? Oh, yeah ...

MR BARRETT: The orange?

SANDY: Yeah ...

MR BARRETT: And what about the –

Get a Job!

SANDY: The water's on the boil.

MR BARRETT: Right. Good. I'll get me coat, then ...

SANDY: You'll need to get some more coffee – the tin's nearly empty.

MR BARRETT: Empty? Flipping 'eck, Sandra, I only opened it last week; that's you, that is, giving away free coffees to all your mates. I wouldn't mind but you're drinking me out of business ... Are you listening?

SANDY: Hey?

MR BARRETT: This is supposed to be a café, you know, not a pigging drop-in centre for Doncaster's unemployed.

SANDY: What?

MR BARRETT: Never mind reading that letter. If your mother sees those chairs are still on the tables you'll be for it ... Sandra ...

SANDY: All right, keep your hair on.

MR BARRETT: What is it, anyroad? Two free tickets for a fortnight's holiday in Rio de Janeiro? 'Just tick the box provided and we'll do all the rest ...'

SANDY: It's from the YTS.

MR BARRETT: The YTS? What do they want?

SANDY: Aw, nothing, it's just a circular.

MR BARRETT: That's where the money's going that I pay in taxes ... sending round circulars to three million unemployed. You'd think they'd find a cheaper way of communicating with folk, wouldn't you. I mean, you're down there every fortnight signing on, why can't they stick all their bits of useless information on a notice-board or something ... save the country a fortune in postage ... I bet it's First Class.

SANDY: First Class.

MR BARRETT: What did I tell you? They want their flipping heads examining. Look at when you first signed on, you got three letters, all arrived the same day, all saying exactly the same thing – nowt. No wonder the country's going to the dogs.

SANDY: That's computers, that is.

MR BARRETT: Computers! They're more bother than they're worth. That's the one decent thing about this game – they can't bring computers into it. Oh no, we're safe in catering, about the only thing that is . . . no substitute for the human touch, you see.

SANDY: They are, though.

MR BARRETT: Eh?

SANDY: It was on the telly a while back; they showed this robot-waiter that took your orders. Mum thought it were great.

MR BARRETT: You're joking!

SANDY: She rang up to find out how much they cost!

MR BARRETT: You what?

SANDY: 'S'true. They told her that it were still in the experimental stage, and that modifications were still needed.

MR BARRETT: Robot flipping waiters?

SANDY: She were a bit put out, though; they told her: 'Costs would be prohibitive to a small family concern such as your own, Mrs Barrett.' She were really cheesed off. She spent the rest of the day sulking. I couldn't believe it.

MR BARRETT: Your mother! I can just picture a robot-waiter let loose in here. Banging into me tables, chipping the formica, dripping oil all over me cushion floor, badgering the customers – mind you, that's not such a bad idea, it might get your mates to pay for their coffees once in a while.

(*Enter* MRS BARRETT.)

MRS BARRETT: Haven't you gone yet? There'll be nothing left by the time that you get up there.

MR BARRETT: I'm just fetching me coat.

MRS BARRETT: Bread's by the back door. Bung it in the freezer, will you?

MR BARRETT: Okey-doke!

(MR BARRETT *goes out.*)

MRS BARRETT: Come on, Sandra, you haven't started yet. It's past nine, you know. I heard it on the radio.

SANDY: All right . . .

MRS BARRETT: Come on, someone might have seen the tables with the chairs on 'em and cleared off somewhere else.

SANDY: No one's been looking.

MRS BARRETT: You never know. Sandra!

SANDY: All right, I'm doing it!

MRS BARRETT: Well hurry up, someone's coming in . . .

(Enter PETE, *Sandy's boyfriend.)*

SANDY: S'all right, it's only Pete.

MRS BARRETT: That's all we need, you come to litter the place up. Tea, is it?

PETE: Oh, ta very much. You're a bit behind, aren't you? It's gone nine.

SANDY: Don't you start! What you up so early for, anyway? You don't normally surface till after dinner.

PETE: Me mam brought me a letter up. Before she went off to work. I've got a job.

MRS BARRETT: Well, congratulations, Peter!

PETE: Starting Monday.

MRS BARRETT: I am glad.

PETE: Pay day Friday!

MRS BARRETT: I am pleased.

PETE: You're not the only one! I was beginning to think I'd be signing on for life.

MRS BARRETT: Here y'are, on the house . . .

PETE: Ta very much, Mrs Barrett . . . Good, eh, Sand?

SANDY: Yeah, it's great. What sort of job is it?

PETE: I'm not sure exactly, I find out more when I turn up on Monday.

SANDY: Turn up where?

PETE: Collins's.

MRS BARRETT: Collins's?

SANDY: On the industrial estate.

PETE: Sort of a warehouse.

SANDY: You'll be packing shelves.

PETE: I don't know what I'm doing.

SANDY: I do. They have vacancies every year. Same jobs. Jackie was there last year, remember, and Si Dutton. It's a YTS, innit.

PETE: Yeah.

MRS BARRETT: YTS?

PETE: Youth Training Scheme.

SANDY: Only there isn't much training in it! You know, you do a full-time job for part-time pay, save the firm a packet, an' at the end of the year it's back on the dole and the firm takes on three more trainees.

PETE: It's still a job, Sand.

SANDY: There's jobs and jobs.

MRS BARRETT: It's all good experience.

SANDY: What? Packing shelves? Very useful if he gets an interview with a garage! It'll help a lot when it comes to changing the oil-filter on an Escort.

PETE: You dunno, it might be something different.

SANDY: Come off it, Pete, you know that's what you'll be doing.

MRS BARRETT: Well, at least it's something more than you can say for some these days ...

SANDY: Meaning me, I suppose. Look, I may not have an actual job but I work hard enough running this café for you and Dad. But you won't catch me jumping in at Collins's just because it's a so-called job.

PETE: What d'you mean, so-called?

MRS BARRETT: I still think you're being very unfair, Sandra. After all, it is a job, no matter what you say, and if it means he won't have to sign on again ...

SANDY: Not until next year, anyway ... An' what's so wrong with signing on? The way you talk you'd think it was leprosy or something.

MRS BARRETT: Yes, we all know it suits you, Sandra.

SANDY: I don't want to sign on. I would quite like a job. I'd much prefer doing a useful job that I liked and enjoyed doing and that I got a decent wage for as well ...

MRS BARRETT: Oh, wouldn't we all!

SANDY: But I'm not gonna do just anything. I'm not selling meself short. I've done what everybody wanted; I worked hard at school ...

PETE: Huh!

SANDY: Yes I did. Dead hard. And I passed me exams. Just so's I could get a good job. Well, where is it, then? I've done my bit. An' I don't see why I should accept a place on a crappy

Youth Training Scheme just because someone's cocked it up!

MRS BARRETT: Well I'm very pleased for you, Peter, even if she isn't. I'd better make a start with those accounts. We had another letter from the VAT man yesterday.

(MRS BARRETT *goes off.* SANDRA *turns to* PETE *in disgust.*)

SANDY: You see! She doesn't even listen.

PETE: Well, you do go on a bit . . .

SANDY: Oh, do I?

PETE: I don't want to doss around. I want to get somewhere, and this is a start.

SANDY: This café's a start for me, too. (*Snapping back*) And it's not dossing either!

PETE: All right, Sand, only we can't all pick an' choose, you know. We can't all have ten-thousand-a-year jobs, ride round in flashy sports cars an' have villas in the South of France . . .

SANDY: I don't want a villa in the South of France. I can't speak French to start with, so fat lot of good that'd do me.

PETE: You needn't live there; you could rent it out to tourists an' holidaymakers, you'd rake in a fortune without doing anything!

SANDY: I don't want to rake in a fortune . . . I'm not interested in making thousands . . . I just want what I deserve. I've done what they all wanted – Mam, Dad, Gran, teachers, me brother, everybody – 'Work hard at school, pass your exams so's you can get a good job.' Well, I've done all that. I stayed in nights doing me homework, revising, slaving over the fishing industry in Denmark and the causes of the First World War – while me mates were down the club, going to discos, parties . . .

PETE: You've been out!

SANDY: Not as much as I could have. I missed out on all that so that I'd do well in me exams . . . get a *good* job, not a bloody YTS for twenty odd quid a week, filling shelves in Collins's warehouse.

PETE: Well, it's not you that's gonna be doing it, is it?

SANDY: No ... Remember when you was little, and people used to say to you, 'What do you want to be when you grow up?' And you could say anything, anything at all – a vet, a nurse, even a train driver! Anything you wanted, and that's what you were going to be ... That was before you found out about exams, and you found that suddenly you couldn't do anything – couldn't be a vet 'cos you haven't got the right pieces of paper – and now you can't be a nurse due to the fact that they're closing down the hospitals! And when you think ... when you were little, you never dreamt of anything stopping you, never thought for a moment that you wouldn't be able to be a vet. 'What do you want to be when you grow up?' That's a laugh!

(*Enter* MR BARRETT *with his coat on.*)

MR BARRETT: Oh, hello, Pete. Where's your mam, Sandra?

SANDY: Upstairs working on the books.

MR BARRETT: Right ... Finally happened, has it?

SANDY: What?

MR BARRETT: I don't know. You tell me. You're the one with the long face.

SANDY: Pete's got a job ...

MR BARRETT: Oh dear, I am sorry, that's really terrible, that is. What can I say? Shall I send flowers or shall I donate the money to a good cause?

SANDY: Keep practising the act, Dad ...

MR BARRETT: Got yourself a job, hey? Congratulations, lad. What is it then? Stunt-man in blue movies?

PETE: It's at Collins's warehouse.

SANDY: Stacking shelves.

MR BARRETT: Well then, when do you start?

PETE: Monday, first thing.

MR BARRETT: Working man at last, hey? (*To* SANDRA) Well, what are you so down in the mouth about?

PETE: 'Cause it's a YTS job. She says it's not a proper job.

MR BARRETT: Oh, she's only jealous. If it were her that was offered it she'd jump at the chance, YTS or no YTS.

SANDY: Fat chance!

Get a Job!

MR BARRETT: It means a lot to a person, going to work, earning your first pay packet ...

SANDY: For what it's worth!

MR BARRETT: Work isn't just about money, Sandra.

SANDY: Well, the YTS certainly isn't!

MR BARRETT: It's about self-respect, responsibility, to others as well as yourself ... being a useful member of society ...

SANDY: Oh aye, very useful is that, stacking bloody shelves!

MR BARRETT: It'll stand him in good stead for when he's looking for other jobs, after he's finished his YTS.

SANDY: After he's served his time, you mean.

MR BARRETT: All good experience.

SANDY: Oh I'm sure ... (*She acts an imaginary interview between* PETE *and an employer*) 'And what experience do you have, Mr Peter Lawson?'

'Oh well, I'm a very experienced and qualified shelf-filler.'

'Oh well, you're just the man we want, we've got a few shelves here that want filling. When can you start?'

PETE: Oh, you're twisting it ...

MR BARRETT: Oh, she will. (*To* SANDY) But doing this year'll give him more chance of getting a job at the end of it; an employer'll look more kindly on him knowing he's done summat with his time, and at least they'll know he can get up in the mornings!

PETE: I don't know what you're so fussed about, Sand, it's only a year after all!

SANDY: Oh, suit yourself!

MR BARRETT: Happen she'll think twice about it when she's offered a place.

SANDY: Think so?

MR BARRETT: You'll jump at it.

SANDY: Think so?

MR BARRETT: Yes, I do.

SANDY: Well, you're wrong then, aren't you.

MR BARRETT: We'll wait and see when the time comes.

SANDY (*taking out letter*): why wait?

MR BARRETT: What's that?

SANDY: Letter I got this morning. Remember? The one with my name on the front ...

MR BARRETT: That circular?

SANDY: Yeah; only it's norra circular, but it is from the YTS.

PETE: Collins's!

SANDY: Yep.

PETE: You got one as well.

MR BARRETT: You mean ... well, why didn't you tell us? Me and your mam?

SANDY: 'Cos you'd expect me to take it, the pair of you, pressure me to take it.

MR BARRETT: Well, you're going to, aren't you? I mean ... what'll happen if you don't take it?

PETE: They'll stop your benefit.

SANDY: Then I'll have to do without. I earn me keep working here in the café.

MR BARRETT: But you can't stay working in here all your life. You need to get yourself a proper job.

SANDY: Like at Collins's? I'd rather work here than there any day of the week ... an' I'll keep looking for work – proper work, work I want to do, work I deserve. An' I'll help you out here while I find it.

PETE: You could get into trouble, Sand, not taking it ... an' it's only for a year.

SANDY: I've got better things to do with my time.

(*Enter* MRS BARRETT.)

MRS BARRETT: What's going on here, then? Teddybears' tupperware party? No wonder this business is making a loss when two thirds of the staff spend all their time chatting with the customers ... sorry, customer.

MR BARRETT: Are you going to tell her?

SANDY: It makes no difference, I'll not do it.

MRS BARRETT: Not do what? What's going on?

MR BARRETT: It's Sandra. She's been offered a job.

SANDY: Some job!

MRS BARRETT: Sandra has? I thought that were you, Pete?

PETE: Me and Sandra both.

MR BARRETT: At Collins's warehouse, the same ...

PETE: The same as me.

MR BARRETT: Starting Monday.

PETE: Pay day Friday!

MRS BARRETT: That's a stroke of good luck ... well, isn't it?

MR BARRETT: She says ... she says she's not going ...

MRS BARRETT: Don't talk daft. Course she's going ... aren't you, love? Sandra? Well, she can't not go, can she? Won't she get into trouble if she refuses? Sandra? SANDRA?

SANDY: Oh God!

(SANDY *storms off.*)

Blackout.

BATTLE LINES

CHARACTERS

SANDY

PETE

MR BARRETT

MRS BARRETT

Family Frictions

SCENE 1 *The Barretts' café.*

SANDY *Barrett comes in with a tray full of washed cups and saucers, which she puts down on the counter.*

SANDY: Eight o'clock! Last customer went at half-six, but you've still to do all the clearing and cleaning. It's slave labour in 'ere. And it don't help that it's your mam and dad that's employin' yer. Still, it's work, innit? There's thousands wouldn't mind it. Just get finished, then I'm off out to Pete. 'Your Young Man' as they call him.

MR BARRETT (*off*): Sandra? Who's that in there?

SANDY: No one, Dad!

MR BARRETT: No one? Well, don't talk to yerself then. They'll put yer away.

SANDY: It'd be a rest cure compared to this slaving.

MR BARRETT (*entering*): I heard that! What's up wi' you then?

SANDY: Nothing.

MR BARRETT: Nothing? Well, you're the only one in the world can say *that*. Money, is it?

SANDY: Suppose so.

MR BARRETT: You're the one wouldn't go on the YTS. You made yer bed, now you lie on it.

(*He glances off, takes out a fiver and puts it in front of her.*)

SANDY: A fiver, Dad?

MR BARRETT: Don't tell yer mam!

SANDY: Why?

MR BARRETT: She'll say I'm spoilin' yer.

SANDY: She spoiled Richard when he was home.

MR BARRETT: Well, he's not home. He's half way round the world in a submarine. Now do me a favour. Go and fetch up one o' them big tins of coffee.

SANDY: Is that it, then?

MR BARRETT: Yes. Meeting your young man tonight?

SANDY: Yeh. He's been to the match. I'm meeting him outside the ground.

MR BARRETT: Watch yerself in them football crowds. Flamin' 'ooligans!

SANDY: I know – don't give us yer speech, Dad.

MR BARRETT: I don't understand it, I really don't. It never used to be like it is now.

SANDY: 'Ere we go. The Speech!

MR BARRETT: Something's happened. There was pleasure, real pleasure in my young day, to go to football. It were the top o' the week. It were . . . pride. Stickin' together. Even in bad times.

SANDY: Dad . . .

MR BARRETT: I know. You'll say that was years ago, before you were born. But you tell me where it's all gone wrong.

SANDY: Well . . .

MR BARRETT: I'll tell you where it's gone wrong. We went soft. I'm sorry to say it, but we went soft, our lot, on yours. We should've put our foot down hard, early on. Before it took hold. No good doin' all this short sharp shock stuff now. Too late! Course it is. We shoulda cracked down on yer early on.

SANDY: Dad!

MR BARRETT: Eh?

SANDY: Yer talkin' about *me*, are yer?

MR BARRETT: Course not. Yer a girl for a start.

SANDY: There's girl football hooligans.

MR BARRETT: Don't tell me, I don't wanna know. Just do what I say, an' watch yerself in them crowds.

SANDY: OK. I'll pay yer back this if Pete pays. He usually does.

MR BARRETT: He's not hard up, then. Where's it come from?

SANDY: His mam and dad, I think. He likes to keep smart.

MR BARRETT: You keep hold of that, anyway. Now go and get that coffee tin, will yer?

(MRS BARRETT *comes into the café.*)

MRS BARRETT: Oh, Sandra, I'm glad you're still here.

SANDY: Oh, Mum, I've done all the jobs. I'm supposed to meet Pete in ten minutes.

MRS BARRETT: I've just heard on the radio. There's been a fight up at the football ground. Some kind of riot.

MR BARRETT: 'Ell-fire . . .

SANDY: Pete can look after himself, don't worry.

MRS BARRETT: Make sure he looks after *you*, that's all I ask, love.

15

SANDY: Don't worry, Mum!
MRS BARRETT: You wait till you have children, love, then you'll know what worry means.
SANDY: Children! I've only just left school, Mum!

(*She leaves to fetch the coffee tin.*)

MRS BARRETT: She'll be all right, won't she?
MR BARRETT: Anybody tries it on'll be answerable to me.
MRS BARRETT: Pete'll look after her, I'm sure. He's got a bit of backbone, that boy. He's got a bit of pride. In himself. Not like some you read about.

(SANDY *re-enters with the coffee tin, puts it on the counter.*)

SANDY: Right. I've done. See yer later! (*She picks up her coat and goes to the door, where she turns*) Cheer up! It may never happen.

(*She exits.*)

SCENE 2   *A park bench.*

Police car sirens are heard in the distance. SANDY *enters.*

SANDY: Two hours I waited for 'im! Two whole boring hours, watching the sky go dark. Watching police vans belting up and down, watching people watching me, thinking, 'What's that tart standin' around for?' So you can guess, when 'is Lordship showed up, I weren't too pleased.

(*Enter* PETE *in smart, but slightly ruffled, casual clothes. There's a bruise on his face.*)

SANDY: What the bloody 'ell time d'you call this?
PETE: Sand . . . I'm sorry.
SANDY: I should bloody well think so! I've been stood here waiting for you two hours!
PETE: Leave it till tomorrow, eh? I feel terrible.
SANDY: Like 'ell I'll leave it – what've you done to your face?
PETE: Nothing.

(*She puts her hand up to his bruise.*)

PETE: Ow! Don't touch it!

SANDY: Someone's 'it yer. Pete, love, who was it?

PETE: Kids from the other side. Bastards. Cornered us, tried to do us in.

SANDY: What 'other side'? The other team's lot?

PETE: Sort of ... Leave it now, eh? I'm goin' home.

SANDY: Get a doctor.

PETE: No. Forget it.

SANDY: I will not. You might have concussion. Look promise me you'll see a doctor. I'd take you meself, but we're off out tomorrow, to me aunty's.

PETE: OK ... OK ... I'll see yer, right?

SANDY: Come round Monday, then.

PETE: Can't. Not Monday.

SANDY: Why?

PETE: I can't.

SANDY: Why, Pete?

PETE: I've got to go to court.

SANDY: Court? What for?

PETE: Assault.

SANDY: Bloomin' 'eck, love, it's you's been assaulted!

PETE: Yeah, well ...

SANDY: I'm comin' with yer, then.

PETE: No you're not.

SANDY: I am, I'm comin' with yer!

PETE: I said 'No!' I don't want you there!

SANDY: Why? I'm yer girlfriend, I want to be there.

PETE: Look, do me a favour, will yer. I don't want you in court, right? So stop at home. Please. Do we have to stand 'ere, me 'ead's splittin' ...

SANDY: I'm sorry, love. I'll walk home with yer. You'll feel better tomorrow.

PETE: Iss OK, Sand. Gary's over there with his van. Look, I'll come round yours on Monday, after, OK?

SANDY: But what if ... ? What if they ... ?

PETE: They won't! The Platoon Cannot Be Beat, remember?

SANDY: The what?

PETE: The Platoon.

SANDY: What the 'ell's that?

PETE: It's what we call ourselves. I thought you knew.
SANDY: 'Platoon'? How long's this been going on?
PETE: Coupla years.
SANDY: What is it?
PETE: It's our mob.
SANDY: *Who* is?
PETE: Kids who used to know each other at school. Few others.
Look, why the questions? Don't worry!
SANDY: Why d'yer call yerselves 'The Platoon'?
PETE: Talk about it Monday, eh? Come 'ere. (*He pulls her to him,
so that his back is to the audience*) Promise me you won't go to
court Monday. Promise?
SANDY: Promise. (*We see her crossing her fingers. Addressing the
audience*) Yeah, I know it were a rotten trick, crossing me
fingers, but there were something going on that I had to
know about. Anyway, back to the action – no point depriv-
ing meself, was there?

(*She goes to give* PETE *a passionate kiss, but she accidentally
touches his bruise. He yells and pulls back.*

PETE: Ah! Bloody 'ell, Sand. Watchit will yer!
SANDY: Oh, God, I'm sorry, I forgot.
PETE: I'm off, right. I'll come round your place after. Wearing a
suit of armour!
SANDY: Oh, very sexy!
PETE: Yeah, I am, aren't I? Ta-ra!

(*He exits.*)

SANDY: 'Platoon'. I thought: What's 'e think 'e's in? The Army?
I got me answer Monday, in court.

(*Police car sirens heard in the distance*).

SCENE 3   *Empty café.*

PETE *enters, looks around, goes to the counter and pours himself a
cup of tea which he takes to a table. He seems confident and cocky.*
MRS BARRETT *appears at the counter.*

MRS BARRETT: Oh, hello, Peter! I don't know where she's got to, Peter love. She said she were goin' shoppin'.

PETE: Don't matter, Mrs Barrett. Tell yer what, give us an apple pie, eh?

(He goes up to the counter. She puts a square packet on a plate for him. He forgets to pay, partly because he's started chuckling to himself.)

MRS BARRETT: You what, love?

PETE: Oh. Nothing, Mrs Barrett.

(He tries to suppress his excited laughter, but can't.)

MRS BARRETT: You're very cheerful.

PETE: Am I? Oh, yeah. Well, it's been a funny day, has today.

MRS BARRETT: Funny ha-ha?

PETE: Beg yer pardon, love?

MRS BARRETT: Or funny peculiar?

PETE: Oh. Bit of both, really.

MRS BARRETT: Well, *we* had a bit of drama here, Saturday, I can tell you.

PETE: Oh? What were that then?

MRS BARRETT: We had three football hooligans in here.

(PETE chokes on his tea.)

MRS BARRETT: Yes. I thought that might surprise you. Three of 'em.

PETE: Er ... local, were they?

MRS BARRETT: No! They'd come up on the train. For the match. But they weren't allowed in, they said.

PETE: So you talked to 'em, then?

MRS BARRETT: Yes, I did. Why not? They're human beings!

PETE: Are they? Hah ...

MRS BARRETT: You may say it's wrong, Peter, I know I'm a bit old-fashioned, but I happen to think we'll never change these people unless we talk to them. It's no good ranting on about locking them up, and bringing back the birch and National Service, like Eddie does. It'd make things worse. Violence breeds violence, doesn't it? Take all this going on in Beirut, now, I mean –

Family Frictions

PETE: Mrs B.?

MRS BARRETT: Yes, love?

PETE: They didn't – these lads – they weren't looking for anyone? Were they?

MRS BARRETT: No, love, I don't think so. Looking for who?

PETE: Oh, I dunno. No one.

MRS BARRETT: They were quite nice, really. *And* they paid up.

PETE: Eh? Oh, sorry, the apple pie ... Here ...

(*He offers her money.*)

MRS BARRETT: No, love, I didn't mean you. My treat.

(*She goes back behind the counter.*)

PETE: Ey-up, Mrs Barrett. What's that out there? Starin' in at us. In the dark glasses and the hat?

MRS BARRETT: Oh my God ... Oh, silly! It's Sandra. Whatever's she playing at?

PETE: Here she comes.

(*Door opens.* SANDY *comes in.* PETE *waves a hand in front of her face.*)

PETE: Hello! Anyone in? It's me, Pete. Fancy a bite of me apple pie?

(*She takes off her dark glasses. Her expression is grim.*)

MRS BARRETT: That's better, love. Now we can see your face. Did you get yer shopping?

SANDY: Shopping?

MRS BARRETT: Yer shopping. Yer went for.

SANDY: Oh ... yeah.

MRS BARRETT: Though why you have to dress up like Mata Hari, I don't know.

PETE: Dark glasses make you mysterious, Mrs Barrett.

MRS BARRETT: Well, she can be mysterious behind this counter for a bit. Yer dad's down the Cash and Carry, love, and there's the VAT man coming, so I've the books to do. Would you mind?

SANDY: No. It'll give me an' 'im a chance to talk.

MRS BARRETT: Oh yes, that'll be nice.

PETE: Yeah. Very nice. I think . . .

(MRS BARRETT *exits.*)

PETE: Here I am. Large as life.
SANDY: Twice as ugly.
PETE: Ta. Well?
SANDY: Well what?
PETE: Don't you wanna know 'ow it went?
SANDY: How did it?
PETE: Cracked it!
SANDY: Oh?
PETE: Told you we would. The Platoon cannot be beat, right?
SANDY: Yeah, yeah. So tell me. What happened?
PETE: We pleaded not guilty. So he let us off. The Law didn't half look sick!
SANDY: And?
PETE: And what?
SANDY: What else did the magistrate say?
PETE: Nothing. Come on, let's go out.
SANDY: No, I've to stop here. And so've you.
PETE: No! Better things to do, me.
SANDY: Did you look round the court when you were stood there?
PETE: Yeah. So what?
SANDY: So you didn't see someone in dark glasses sat at the back?
PETE: No. Who was . . . ? *You?*
SANDY: Right.
PETE: You! I told you not to come! I bloody said, 'Don't come!'
SANDY: Well I did. And I heard all about the precious Platoon, and how you lot put one of the other team's supporters in hospital with a fractured skull.
PETE: Spyin' on me, Sand!
SANDY: Heard the police say you were 'disciplined', 'well-organised', 'well-dressed'!
PETE: Yeah, well, it were that bit that got us off, I reckon.
SANDY: And I heard you claim you were set on by the – what? – the South Gate Mob?
PETE: We were.

SANDY: It was planned. You'd both planned it!

PETE: So what's the problem? We got off!

SANDY: You got off because that flamin' magistrate was conned. All that stuff about defending yourselves, innocent football fans protecting themselves against hooligans from outside town! You conned 'im *You're* the hooligans.

PETE: Never!

SANDY: Yes!

PETE: Look, Sand, it's war.

SANDY: It's what?

PETE: War! Platoon's always taken on the South Gate Mob. It's tradition. We're old enemies.

SANDY: Why?

PETE: Why? I dunno. They probably started callin' us names, we called 'em back. Someone goes like that with 'is arm, someone chucks something. Then before y'know where you are, it's World War Three!

SANDY: And all those Saturdays I thought you were off watching football, yer not, yer smashin' 'ell out of each other, right?

PETE: They do it to us, we do it to them. I told yer. It's a war.

SANDY: I can't believe I'm hearin' this!

PETE: All right, Sand, your brother, he's in the Navy, right? He went down the Falklands in 'is submarine. Coulda got isself blown out the water by the Argies. That's war. But yer don't mind that, 'cos you've got pride. Yer've got mates around yer. All for one an' one for all.

SANDY: No one's bombin' *you*!

PETE: They're chuckin' all sorts at us! Lumps o' concrete, iron bars, the lot!

SANDY: They're English. They're not invadin' yer, Pete, for God's sake! Are they?

PETE: They are. Invadin' our territory. Everyone knows there's Platoon territory. And there's South Gate Mob territory. You go to get a bit of theirs, and defend a bit of yours.

SANDY: And what about ordinary people who get caught in the middle? Little kids seeing your fancy Platoon marching about in bovver boots?

PETE: It's always gotta be 'bovver boots', hasn't it? We don't wear 'em. Never have. We're smart, we wear casuals –

SANDY: I don't care if you wear plastic bags on yer 'eads! Yer still actin' like ... like hooligans!

PETE: Yer don't understand anything about it.

SANDY: Dead right I don't! (*Pause*) Why, Pete, why?

PETE: Look ... you feel good, why else? You've *done* something – *if* you win, which we do most of the time. You feel ... you feel you could do *any*thing, sometimes. When yer all together. Feeling strong. Alive. All of you. Ask yer flamin' brother, he'd know.

SANDY: Leave Richard out of it, there's no comparison.

PETE: No? When his lot do it, they get medals. When it's us, they try and send us down.

SANDY: Completely different. That was war – *real* war. Our country sent him. They're not askin' *you* to pick fights every Saturday afternoon, scare people stupid.

PETE: They didn't ask Richard if he wanted to go and fight the Argies, did they?

SANDY: You do it for fun!

PETE: Don't tell me some o' *them* didn't enjoy themselves.

SANDY: Oh! ... I give up. Yer like a schoolboy, you are. Still scrappin' in the playground. Haven't grown up.

PETE: So having guts, and pride, planning it all out, strategy, thinking, that's all kids' stuff is it? Well, so is Richard a kid, then!

SANDY: That's my brother you're talkin' about!

PETE: Look, I respect Richard. We're both ... like ... warriors, me an' 'im.

SANDY: Oh yeah? Then join the Army, like the magistrate said.

PETE: Not the Army. He told us we should join the Territorials, remember? (*Imitates*) 'They need young lads of energy and courage, prepared to stand up for themselves.'

SANDY: You were lucky to get off, that's all I can say.

PETE: I know. Only 'cos we looked right to 'im. Eh, shall I join the Scouts, shall I?

SANDY: Don't see what's so funny ...

PETE: Tell yer one thing. I wouldn't join th' Army.

SANDY: Why?

PETE: Be away from you, wouldn't I?

SANDY: Oh. Great.

PETE: I mean it. Yer still my girl, right.

SANDY: Not if this Platoon crap carries on.

PETE: We could get married.

SANDY: What?

PETE: Er . . . one day.

SANDY: Oh yeah? And what d'we do on honeymoon? Invade the hotel next door, beat the guests to pieces, and come 'ome wi' bits of plumbin' as souvenirs?

PETE: I'm not stupid, Sand.

SANDY: No?

(*A tense silence.* MR *and* MRS BARRETT *come in.*)

MRS BARRETT: Right, love, we're both back. You can go now if yer want to.

MR BARRETT: All right, young Peter? Hey, tell yer what, I were readin' about that match last Saturday. Sounded a cracker! I were thinkin' — I might go meself next week. Thought we might, you know, make up a party.

SANDY: Well, don't forget to wear yer casuals then, will yer, Dad!

(*She storms out of the room.*)

MRS BARRETT: Sandra . . .

MR BARRETT: Sorry. Did I say summat wrong?

(PETE *stands, awkwardly, between the* BARRETTS.)

Blackout.

END OF THE ROAD

CHARACTERS

SANDY

GRANDAD

MRS BARRETT

MR BARRETT

Family Frictions

SCENE *Evening. The Barretts' kitchen. It has a back door and a hallway leading off.*

GRANDAD *enters by the back door. He wears slippers and limps heavily. He gives a disgruntled snort as he surveys the breakfast dishes on the kitchen table. He sits and begins to read a newspaper. We hear the front door open and shut.* GRANDAD *doesn't look up.* SANDY *enters and he pointedly continues reading.*

SANDY: Hi, Grandad.

GRANDAD: Oh, it's you. Where's your mother and father?

SANDY: Still at the café. It's been murder. On the go all day.

GRANDAD (*sour*): That makes a change.

SANDY (*taking off coat*): Here, I saw you out back talking to old Miss Hemsley.

GRANDAD: Been on a march, she had, to the Houses of Parliament.

SANDY: Miss Hemsley!

GRANDAD: 'Fighting for our rights, Mr Barrett,' she said. 'Rights for over-sixties.'

SANDY: What'd she do? Burn her bra or summat?

GRANDAD: No respect, have you?

SANDY: I think she fancies you. Last chance to get hitched before she snuffs it.

GRANDAD: There's a tamer laid up for you, young lady.

SANDY: So you keep saying. I'm going to the front room. It's time for my series.

GRANDAD: You can't watch that.

SANDY: You're not going to bed already! I suppose I could move the telly in here, into the kitchen.

GRANDAD: I'm not going to bed. I'm watching snooker.

SANDY: But it's my series!

GRANDAD: You've got your whole life to be watching these series of yours.

SANDY: But Grandad, I told you this morning I wanted to watch it.

GRANDAD: And I'm telling you I'm watching snooker. I'm entitled to watch a bit of telly at my age. Not much to ask.

SANDY: I come back specially to watch it. It's not fair.

GRANDAD: Instead of watching telly, you should be giving

your mother a hand, get that washing up done. It's been there since breakfast. I don't know what sort of house this is.

SANDY: I've been working at the café since eight this morning. So's Mum and Dad.

GRANDAD: You don't know what work is, lass. (*Going*) Young people, you've no idea.

SANDY (*to herself*): Damn! Damn and blast!

(*We hear the front door open and shut.*)

SANDY: That'll be Mum and Dad. I suppose I'd better get started on this.

(*She starts washing up.* MR *and* MRS BARRETT *come into the hall.*)

MRS BARRETT: I did tell you, Eddie. Bring two pints of milk, because we've none at home.

(MR *and* MRS BARRETT *come into the kitchen.*)

MR BARRETT: If you did, I didn't hear you. I was doing the accounts. Hullo, love.

SANDY: Hi.

MR BARRETT (*to* MRS BARRETT): I don't know why we keep running out of milk anyway.

MRS BARRETT: It's with Dad here –

MR BARRETT: Then order extra. It's simple enough.

MRS BARRETT: Why can't you do it? Why's it got to be me?

SANDY: Happy families again, is it?

MRS BARRETT: And you might have got this cleared up, Sandra.

SANDY: I've only just got in. And I have started. (*She attacks washing up.*)

MRS BARRETT (*genuine*) I'm sorry, love. Eddie, maybe I didn't tell you about the milk . . . I don't know, I'm so tired these days.

MR BARRETT: Here, sit yourself down.

(GRANDAD *enters.*)

MR BARRETT: Hullo, Dad. How's the leg?

GRANDAD: Same as when you asked me yesterday.

MRS BARRETT: You're looking better. More colour.

GRANDAD: I'll have my cocoa, Ann, now you're back.

MRS BARRETT: It'll have to be tinned milk. We've run out of fresh.

GRANDAD: Run out of milk? No wonder that café's going bankrupt. Told you you'd not make a go of it.

MR BARRETT (*unruffled*): There's plenty of milk at café, and we're not going bankrupt.

SANDY: Anyway, it's nothing to do with you, Grandad.

MRS BARRETT (*reprimanding*): Sandra. Will you have that cocoa, Dad?

GRANDAD: Tinned milk. I don't like it. (*Going*) I'll do without.

(*He leaves.*)

SANDY: Too bad when he had that fall, he didn't break his neck.

MR BARRETT (*laughs*): He doesn't mean any harm, love. Just his way.

MRS BARRETT: It's hard for him. He misses your gran.

SANDY: I doubt she misses him. Probably died to get away from him.

MRS BARRETT: Now that's childish. I don't know what's got into you lately, Sandra.

SANDY: It's him, Mum. He gets on me nerves. I tell people I've got me grandad staying, because he's been poorly. And they say: 'Oh, that's nice!', just assuming he's a lovely old gentleman, like in a telly advert. They want to try living with him! He upsets everyone. Takes everything for granted. Never says 'thank you'. Like the old lady in the supermarket yesterday. I stood there, held the door open for her. Walked right past, not a word, not even a smile. Old people go on about us. They want to take a look at themselves. I hate coming home with him here, Mum. When's he going back to his place?

MRS BARRETT: You'd better tell her Eddie. We were going to tell you at the weekend anyway, love.

MR BARRETT: The fact is, Sandra, we feel, your mother and I, your grandad would be better off here, with us.

SANDY (*horrified*): You don't mean ... not forever, Dad!

MRS BARRETT: He can't cope, love, not on his own.

MR BARRETT: We'd have the spare room done up, so he'd not be sleeping in the front room.

SANDY: But his leg? He can't get upstairs.

MR BARRETT: We'd have a stair-lift put in for him.

MRS BARRETT: He wants to stay. Not that he's said. Too proud.

MR BARRETT: He won't be much trouble, once he's settled.

SANDY: Not much trouble! It's alright for you. It's Mum who gets lumbered.

MR BARRETT: It's up to you and me, then, to see she doesn't.

MRS BARRETT: We'll just have to pull together, do that little bit extra. And that includes you, love.

SANDY: I already help out at the café. And I am supposed to be looking for a proper job. How can I do that, stuck here looking after a geriatric?

MR BARRETT (*laughs*): There's plenty of go in the old man yet!

SANDY: Aye. He could go on forever. But will *we* survive, that's the point!

MRS BARRETT: He can't manage on his own. Even before he fell sick, the state of his flat. And I can't keep on running over. It's too far. I've not the time.

SANDY: He could have one of those home helps. He could manage then.

MR BARRETT: Home helps! They don't come just like that!

SANDY: If he's entitled, he's entitled. It's up to the council.

MR BARRETT: You try telling them that.

MRS BARRETT: At least here we know he's being properly looked after.

SANDY: You're not being realistic, Mum. It's not just me I'm thinking of.

MRS BARRETT (*sceptical*): Oh aye?

SANDY: It's you and Dad as well. With the café, you're up to your eyes as it is. And you hardly ever used to row before he came.

MRS BARRETT: So what do you suggest, then? We put him in a home? Is that it?

SANDY: I hadn't thought of that. Yes. One of those homes.

MRS BARRETT: You'd do that, to your own grandad!

MR BARRETT: You saw that programme on telly.

MRS BARRETT: Heartbreaking.

MR BARRETT: I'd not do that, not to my father, put him in a place like that.

SANDY: They can't all of them be bad.

MRS BARRETT: I can see, Eddie, we've a fine old age to look forward to. Our Sandra, she'll put us in a home. No matter what it's like, as long as she's not bothered.

SANDY: I might not be here to look after you. I might be in London . . . America.

MR BARRETT (*wry*): America, is it?

SANDY: Just tell me, do you want me to stay here all my life, just to look after you in your old age?

MRS BARRETT: I'm sure I'm not one to put anyone out, Sandra.

SANDY: What about Richard, big brother Richard? You were all keen on him going away, on him joining the Navy. Or is it just me, expected to give up my life? My life doesn't count –

MRS BARRETT: Not the feminist stuff. Not now, Sandra, I can't stand it.

SANDY: Mum, what if I can't look after you? What if I'm dead, *and* Richard – it could happen.

MRS BARRETT: Now you're being morbid.

SANDY: What if Grandad didn't have us? What if *your* parents were both alive? Would we be expected to have them all here, dossing all over the house?

MRS BARRETT (*at the end of her tether*): Don't ask, I don't know, how would I know! For heaven's sake, Sandra, you do go on!

MR BARRETT: That's enough, Sandra, you're upsetting your mother.

SANDY: I'm just saying that you can't rely on people. So it's up to the government –

MR BARRETT: If people don't look after their own, I don't know as why the government should.

SANDY: It's what you've paid your stamps for, Dad.

MRS BARRETT: I just hope your children show a little more feeling.

SANDY: I shan't live that long. When I can't look after myself, I'm committing euthanasia.

MR BARRETT (*laughs*): You say that now!

SANDY: What I feel is, when you've had your life, that's it. Don't hang around, mess things up for other people. Get out while the going's good. I'd hate it, to feel I was a burden on my kids.

MRS BARRETT: Happen they'll want to look after you, their own mother.

SANDY: Like you want to look after Grandad? You don't even like him.

MRS BARRETT (*shocked*): What a thing to say!

MR BARRETT: There's bonds. Blood. You'll see.

SANDY: That sentimental stuff, I don't believe in that.

MR BARRETT (*amused*): Got it all worked out then, eh?

SANDY: Having Grandad here, it's made me think about it. I tell you, if he stays – I go!

(GRANDAD *enters, unobserved.*)

MRS BARRETT: Oh dear. Sandra, love –

SANDY: I won't be able to stand it with him here, I just won't. I'll go into that squat with Helen and the others.

GRANDAD: There'll be no need for that.

(SANDY, MR *and* MRS BARRETT *are dismayed, realising they've been overheard.*)

GRANDAD: Come to say I'd have that cocoa. Door were open and –

MRS BARRETT: Sandra, now look what you've done!

GRANDAD: 'What to do with the old man?' A problem for you, in't it?

MR BARRETT (*gentle, reassuring*): Come on now, Dad. It's not like that at all.

GRANDAD: Is it my fault my body's worn out? You think I like it? I tell you this, inside I'm the same Jack Barrett as ever was. A young man trapped in old bones!

SANDY (*upset*): Grandad –

GRANDAD: Hard graft, a life of hard graft, that's what's done it!

MRS BARRETT: Sandra, you apologise, apologise to your grandad –

GRANDAD: Oh, I know what she thinks! Euthanasia. Put the old beggar down!

SANDY: Grandad, no . . . I never meant that –

31

GRANDAD: Euthanasia. Aye, I've thought on't. Better a black box six foot under than left to rot on't scrap heap.

MR BARRETT: Sit yourself down, Dad. I'll get you a tot of summat.

GRANDAD: I'm going back to my flat.

(SANDY, MR *and* MRS BARRETT *protest*.)

GRANDAD: I've got a taxi ordered.

MRS BARRETT (*to herself*): Oh, no.

MR BARRETT: Come on, now. Of course you're not going.

GRANDAD: I've made up my mind, and you'll not alter it.

MRS BARRETT: Dad, you're all upset.

GRANDAD: Not bloody surprising, is it? Born in Great War. 1916. Then, after the war, the Depression. No work. No Youth Training Schemes in them days, neither. Just hunger in your belly. But they had an answer. 'Opportunities,' they said, 'waiting round 't corner.' Aye. The next war. 'Opportunity' to fight for freedom. We fought, and won – my generation. And there was hope. The Welfare State. And for that I worked, paid my stamps, my contribution to the Welfare State. Now here I am, at the end of the road, with a pension I can't live on – scrape by on, just, but not live. I've been had. Senior citizen? Third-class citizen, more like. And waiting on't corner, one of those homes where you lose your wits waiting to die amongst strangers, because your own family –

MR BARRETT: Dad, just drink this, eh? Calm you down. Now listen. Your home is here, with us.

SANDY: They're having a stair-lift put in and everything.

MRS BARRETT: Sandra never meant . . . she loves you, Dad. We all do.

GRANDAD: Words come cheap, Ann. Life's taught me that.

(*The front door bell rings.*)

MR BARRETT: The taxi. I'll send it away.

GRANDAD (*commanding*): No. I warn you, son. It's my taxi, and I'm going in it.

MRS BARRETT: Eddie, don't let him go!

MR BARRETT: I can't stop him. I'll give you a hand, Dad.

GRANDAD: I can manage. (*Going*) I don't need you, nor the government, no one. Never have. Never shall. I'll manage like I always have. On my own.

SANDY (*pleading*): Grandad, please –

GRANDAD: Your turn'll come, lass. I don't envy you. The government's seeing to your future. You'll be lucky if you get a pension! Victorian values. Clock going back. My grandmother died in't workhouse. Seems my grandaughter'll do likewise. (*Going*) I'd be obliged if you'd send my things on.

(*He makes a dignified exit as the others look helplessly on. We hear the front door open.* SANDY *makes a move to run after* GRANDAD.)

MR BARRETT (*restraining*): No, Sandra, let him go.

(*We hear the front door shut.*)

MR BARRETT: I'll give him half an hour, then fetch him back.

SANDY: It's all my fault.

MRS BARRETT: Why's he have to be so . . . (*Crying*) He knows we want the best by him.

SANDY: Don't cry, Mum.

MRS BARRETT: I can see it. There'll be scenes like this with him all the time.

MR BARRETT: He's not easy, I know.

MRS BARRETT: Even with the spare room we'll all be on top of each other. And there's the expense. The stair-lift.

MR BARRETT: Another year till we get the café renovated.

MRS BARRETT: He's your father, I thought of course we'll have him here. It'd be a sacrifice in some ways. But what are families for? But now I'm actually faced with it, Eddie –

SANDY: I'll help you more, Mum. I will.

MR BARRETT: What is it you're saying, Ann? That we shouldn't have him here after all?

SANDY: Mum?

MRS BARRETT (*crying*): I don't know. I just don't know . . .

Fade lights to blackout.

STAND UP AND BE COUNTED

CHARACTERS

SANDY

CAROL

RICHARD

PETE

MR BARRETT

Family Frictions

SCENE 1 *The Barretts' café in a Yorkshire town.*

SANDY *comes in, and puts a tape into the cassette-player. She starts to wipe down surfaces, dry cups, etc.* RICHARD, *her brother, comes in.*

RICHARD: You still listening to that old rubbish?

SANDY: Why do brothers always think they can criticise?

RICHARD: It's me superior brains.

SANDY: If you believe that you'll believe anything. Where's Mum and Dad?

RICHARD: Mum's still in bed. She's got a cold coming on. Dad's still snoring in front of breakfast telly.

SANDY: Typical! When's your train?

RICHARD: Couple of hours yet.

SANDY: Where're you off to now? South Sea Islands? Lying on the beach with native girls rubbing your back with sun-oil, I bet.

RICHARD: What? Freezin' in a Force Nine gale up to me ankles in spew, more like!

SANDY: Oh, Richard! D'you 'ave to?

RICHARD: You know I'm not allowed to tell you, so don't ask.

SANDY: Wherever it is, you're lucky. At least you're not stuck in 'ere.

RICHARD: Well, get out, then. You've got to stand up for yerself, Sandra. Do what *you* want, what *you* think's right.

SANDY: Yeah, I know. But what?

RICHARD: Not for me to say, is it? It's for you.

SANDY: Yeah . . .

(PETE *comes in to the café.*)

RICHARD: 'Ey-up! 'Ere it is!

SANDY: Hello, stranger.

PETE: Get us a coffee, will yer, Sand?

SANDY: His last servant died of overwork.

PETE: I'm ill.

RICHARD: You shouldn't have knocked it back so much last night. I warned you.

PETE: I thought you sailor-lads were the hard-drinking lot.

RICHARD: Not me, mate. I've had enough of all that. I'd rather keep me head clear and me body fit these days.

36

Stand up and be counted

PETE: Listen to 'im. Dunnit make yer sick?

SANDY: No. And if you'd any sense you'd do the same. You want coffee, Rich?

RICHARD: Ta.

PETE: And some aspirins.

RICHARD: You shoulda seen 'im, your boyfriend. Up on the table.

SANDY: In the pub?

RICHARD: In the pub. Doin' his tribute to the defenders of our island home, wasn't it, Pete?

SANDY (*laughing*): God in heaven . . . !

RICHARD: Doin' what he thought was a hornpipe. Only it was like he was stuck on Fast Forward!

PETE: I never! . . . Did I?

RICHARD: You did, my son. Very embarrassing it were, too. Till you fell off the table and we got you out before the landlord chucked you out.

(SANDY *brings over two cups of coffee and aspirins for* PETE.)

PETE: Ta.

RICHARD (*parodying*): 'Rule Britannia, Britannia rules the waves, Britons never never never shall be slaves – oi!'

PETE: Give over will yer! I'm dyin' 'ere!

(RICHARD *smiles and takes out a newspaper to read. The café door opens and* CAROL *comes in. She's about Sandy's age, wears an anorak and carries a haversack with some rolled-up posters sticking out. She goes up to the counter where* SANDY *is.*)

SANDY: Yes, please.

CAROL: Hello, Sandra.

SANDY: Hello . . . ?

CAROL: It's Carol. Carol from school.

SANDY: Carol! I didn't recognise yer! Yer look so different. Great to see you! This is Carol I used to be at school with.

PETE: Oh?

SANDY: That's Pete, the one with the deathly pallor and the bloodshot eyes. The Boyfriend.

PETE: Ha-ha.

CAROL: Hello.

SANDY: And that's Richard. The Brother.

CAROL: Hello.

(RICHARD *gets up and shakes hands with* CAROL. *He flirts with her for a moment, holding onto her hand.*)

SANDY: Right, yer can sit down now, Richard. (*To* CAROL) Yer look so different! Lost weight, or what?

CAROL: I have. I decided to take meself in hand. And I'm rushed off me feet these days.

SANDY: What yer doin'? Workin'?

CAROL: I'm training to be a nursery nurse.

SANDY: Brilliant! I love kids. I've got one of me own.

CAROL: Really? A baby? But you're not –

SANDY: He's sittin' over there with his face on the floor.

CAROL: Oh ... I see! Look, Sandra, I've really come to ask a favour. (*She picks up her rucksack and puts it on the counter. She takes out a roll of posters and spreads one out on the counter*) Could you put one of these in your window please?

SANDY (*picking it up*): CND? Bloody 'ell, Carol, I never knew you were into all that kinda stuff. Yer never were at school.

CAROL: No. But I grew up when I left school. Started to think for meself.

SANDY: The one thing I remember about you is you'd never join in anything. You just kept yerself to yerself – not like the rest of us loudmouths. The Mouse, we called you. Remember?

CAROL: I remember. Perhaps it was starting to work with kids. You start to wonder what the point of bringing babies into the world is, if there's not going to be a world for them to grow up in.

SANDY: Don't. I try not to think about all that. Too depressing!

CAROL: Not if you think positively about how to make the world a safer place to be. That's the whole point. That's why we need more members. That's why I want you to put this up.

SANDY: I don't know. I just think there's nothing ordinary people can do. It's the politicians, isn't it?

CAROL: But that's exactly why –

(*A table scrapes as* RICHARD *gets up. He comes across to the counter and picks up the poster.*

RICHARD: I couldn't help overhearing. So this is CND, is it?

CAROL: Yes, that's right ...

RICHARD: I see ... (*He throws the poster back down onto the counter*) Can I say something?

CAROL: Yes. Please.

RICHARD: I'm in the Navy, right.

CAROL: Oh, I didn't –

RICHARD: No, you didn't realise. That's all right. But there's something you oughta be told.

SANDY: Richard ...

RICHARD: I can speak my mind, can't I?

CAROL: Please. Do.

RICHARD: There's people I work with, blokes I'd trust my life with, good people, many of them have got wives and kids too, so they're not mad, bloodthirsty nutcases, right? Now they're just as keen as you on everyone drawing their pensions. But they reckon your lot as the lowest of the low. When they're rattling around in a metal tub thousands of miles from home, freezing cold and throwing up, I can tell you they feel really grateful to know there's nice little goody-goody boys and girls like you going round behind our backs stirring it. All hold hands round the bomber bases and world peace'll start at eleven o'clock precisely? Bloody lunatic. And bloody dangerous an' all.

CAROL: You don't seem to understand ...

RICHARD: 'Ang on, I've not finished yet. And some of 'em feel so good about your pacifist and communist friends kicking 'em in the crutch back 'ome while they try and keep the peace around the world that they'd cheerfully commit murder if they came across one of you on a dark night in a side street.

CAROL: Is that supposed to be a threat?

RICHARD: Up to you, love. Me, I'm a peaceful sort o' bloke, wouldn't hurt a fly. I just thought you'd like to know, that's all.

(*An embarrassed silence.* PETE *stands up.*)

PETE: Rich . . . take it easy, eh?

CAROL: No, he's entitled to say what he thinks.

SANDY: He bloody isn't!

RICHARD: Come on, let's go out.

PETE: Eh? Where to?

RICHARD: Out. A drink.

PETE: They're not open.

RICHARD: Then a walk! Coming?

PETE: Oh. OK. Wait a bit, then.

(RICHARD *leaves the café.* PETE *looks over at* CAROL *and at* SANDRA, *who is furious.*)

PETE: He's a bit . . . been overdoin' it lately.

SANDY: Well yer'd better go and hold his hand then!

PETE: Er . . . right . . .

(*He goes.*)

SANDY: I'm sorry.

CAROL: Oh, don't worry. I've had worse said to me than that, I can tell you.

SANDY: I've never heard him speak like that. He usually keeps things to himself.

CAROL: Well, I'd better go. Will you put the poster up for me?

SANDY: I . . . I'll have to ask Dad. It's his café. Come back when he's surfaced, and see what he says.

CAROL: OK. In the meantime you can have one of these.

SANDY: What's that?

CAROL: Membership form. In case you decide to join.

SANDY: Me? Join?

CAROL: Yes. See yer soon.

SANDY: But I'm not really –

CAROL: Cheers, Sandra.

(CAROL *goes out of the café.* SANDY *holds the form, looks at it for a moment, then exits, still looking at it.*)

SCENE 2 The Barretts' café.

Enter MR BARRETT, *followed by* SANDY.

SANDY: It's on the counter, there, Dad.

MR BARRETT: So I see. (*He picks the CND poster up and reads it with a sceptical air*) Who brought this, did yer say?

SANDY: Carol James, I used to be at school with. Remember?

MR BARRETT: Can't say I do. Can't have it up anyway.

SANDY: Why?

MR BARRETT: That stuff? CND? Do me a favour! What'll our customers think?

SANDY: They might like it.

MR BARRETT: Never! Half of 'em fought in the war. They'll think we've gone macrobiotic or summat.

SANDY: Well, what about the other half?

MR BARRETT: What about them?

SANDY: They might agree with CND!

MR BARRETT: They might have two 'eads an' all. You know my rule, Sandra. No politics. If we lose so much as half a dozen customers a day we'll be broke inside a month. Trade's dodgy enough as it is.

SANDY: You're scared, aren't you?

MR BARRETT: I'm being sensible, love. I'm making certain you and me and your mother get to eat each week.

SANDY: All right, supposing it was a recruiting poster – say for the Navy!

MR BARRETT: That might be a bit different.

SANDY: Why?

MR BARRETT: Not political.

SANDY: Course it is! What about the people who'd stay away 'cos they don't like armaments?

MR BARRETT: There's a lot of that sort round here.

SANDY: What does Mum say?

MR BARRETT: She'll say the same.

SANDY: You haven't asked 'er?

MR BARRETT: No, and I'm not going to. She's in bed wi' flu, and she'll not want pesterin' with stupid business *I* can take care of well enough.

SANDY: I'm going up to ask her.

MR BARRETT: Sandra! yer mam's ill. She's asleep. Leave her be. Besides, she likes having clothes on her back, same as me. Now can we drop the subject, please? Where's Richard?

SANDY: Gone for a walk.

MR BARRETT: Bloody hell-fire, it's chucking it down. He'll miss his train if he's not back soon.

SANDY: He had a row with Carol.

MR BARRETT: Oh. Did he? About Ban-the-Bomb I suppose?

SANDY: Kind of. Peter went with him to try and calm him down.

MR BARRETT: Peter? He'll be putting the boot into some football supporter, won't he?

SANDY: Dad! That's not funny, yer know!

MR BARRETT: All right! Peace! Surrender! This is supposed to be a nice quiet caff, and it's getting more and more like the flaming Houses of Parliament every day!

(*He goes.*)

SANDY (*to audience*): Peace? I thought, You're joking, Dad! One bit of paper, and one person who's sticking out for her principles – and all this starts. Made *me* think anyway. You do worry about the world. Can't help it. Starvation. Comes from working all day wi' food. You think, OK, we feed all them millions out there for another few months, then what? They go back to starvin'. It don't bear thinkin' about. What can I do? No one listens to me, why should they? And why should *I* feel guilty about it? Mind, it might be different if it were me dyin', or whatever. I suppose that's what this . . . (*she picks up the poster*) . . . is all about. I dunno . . . Oh, yeah, Carol came back a bit later, to find out what me Dad said.

(CAROL *comes into the café.*)

CAROL: Hello. I'm back.

SANDY: You're early.

CAROL: Doesn't take people long to say 'No'. Interested?

SANDY: Just looking.

CAROL: What did your Dad say?

SANDY *and* CAROL (*together*): 'No'.

CAROL: I thought as much. Oh well, there's the council estate over the road. Some shops there.

SANDY: I think you ought to try somewhere a bit . . . well . . . smarter.

CAROL: Smarter?

SANDY: There's not much money round here.

CAROL: So it's only the rich, is it, who should be interested in stopping the world blowing up?

SANDY: I didn't mean that!

CAROL: That's what you said.

SANDY: No it isn't! You're obsessed, you are. Come in 'ere and throw the place in ructions. I don't know! And you used to be so quiet!

CAROL: Look, Sandra, I want there to be a world where people can grow up. You know what'll happen when they start this war.

SANDY: When?

CAROL: Sure. When. It'll stay when as long as people like you don't *do* anything.

SANDY: Me? What can I do? I'm not a politician. I might even agree with you, but what's the use? I can't do anything.

CAROL: Of course you can! The world's full of people like you, saying they can't do anything. If they all got together and did something, some small thing, it'd add up. Things would change. You've got to stand up and be counted, Sandra.

SANDY: All right, what about Richard? *He's* doing something. The world's full of people like Richard, too. They're standing up, they're being counted!

CAROL: But that's different!

SANDY: How?

CAROL: Because it . . . ! Because it is! Right and wrong!

SANDY: He thinks *he's* right, and *you're* wrong!

CAROL: Yes, but . . . Oh! I think I'd better be going.

(*Tense stalemate as she rolls up the poster.* PETE *and* RICHARD *enter the café.*)

RICHARD: I'm gonna be late.

SANDY: Quick, go and see our mam.

RICHARD: Right. Where's me bag, I've lost –

SANDY: Go on! We'll find it.

(RICHARD *rushes out at the back.*)

PETE: Where is 'is bag?

SANDY: I don't know.

(*They look for it.*)

SANDY: There! Under the table.

PETE: We got lost.

SANDY: You got him lost, you mean?

PETE: It started peltin'. So we stopped a taxi. Trouble was, the flamin' driver were lost, that's why he picked us up. Talk about the blind leadin' the blind!

SANDY: Typical.

(*Enter* MR BARRETT *and* RICHARD.)

MR BARRETT: No, Mum's upset 'cos she's feelin' poorly. She'll be right as rain in a day or two.

RICHARD: I wish I didn't have to rush. Me bag!

PETE: Here y'are. Send us a card from 'sssh-you-know-where'.

RICHARD: Wouldn't be a secret if I did that, would it, yer berk! Look, stay outa trouble, right? Or I'll send *my* lads in to sort you out. (*To* MR BARRETT) Dad! I'm off, then.

MR BARRETT: Take care, lad. We're thinking of you all the time. Send us letters.

RICHARD: I will. Bye, then, Dad.

MR BARRETT (*shaking hands with* RICHARD): We're proud of you, son.

RICHARD: Give us a kiss then, little sister.

(SANDY *kisses him.*)

RICHARD: Get yourself, y'know, sorted. Eh?

SANDY: I'll try.

(RICHARD *clocks* CAROL, *still sitting rather awkwardly to one side of all this family business.*)

RICHARD: Er ... sorry if I was ... spoke out of turn, like. No offence.

CAROL: That's OK. No offence.

(*They shake hands quickly.*)

RICHARD: I'm bloody late!

PETE (*his punk parody*): 'Rule Britannia, Britannia rule the waves – ah!'

RICHARD: Turn 'im off, someone. See yer!

(*He leaves.*)

MR BARRETT: Come on. Back to work. Can't stand round moping.

(*He leaves.*)

CAROL: I'd better go, too. Sorry if I was in the way.

(*She picks up her rucksack and makes to go.*)

SANDY: Course you weren't. Carol ...
CARCL: Yes?
SANDY: Wait. We ought to talk. Shall we meet ... have a drink?
CAROL: OK. I'll drop by sometime. Sorry if I stirred it up.
SANDY: No! No problem.
CAROL: Bye, then.
SANDY: Bye.

(CAROL *moves to the door.*)

SANDY: Wait! Give us a poster. Go on, quick!

(CAROL *hands her a poster.*)

CAROL: Surprise, surprise. Bye.

(*She leaves.*)

PETE: You'll catch 'ell from your Dad if you put that up. You know that?
SANDY: If I stick it up in 'ere, perhaps. But there's *my* room, *my* window. That's *my* business.
PETE: Oh, come off it, Sand. Yer not really gonna be one o' them CND-ers, are yer? Yer don't believe all that crap, do yer?
SANDY: I don't know, do I?
PETE: It just causes trouble. Yer can see that.
SANDY: Who was it said I'd to stand up for meself? Do what *I* want. Do what *I* think's right. Eh?

PETE: She's just stirrin' it, Sand.
SANDY: It were Richard. Well, maybe he's right. Whatever I decide, it's about bloody time I decided something.

Blackout.

ON THE PILL

CHARACTERS

VANESSA

SANDY

MRS CLAYTHORPE

MRS BARRETT

MR BARRETT

PETE

Family Frictions

SCENE 1 *A bedroom.*

SANDY *and* VANESSA *enter.*

VANESSA: You sit on the chair, Sand. I'll sit on the bed.

SANDY: Your mum's out?

VANESSA: She's at my auntie's. Won't be back for ages. Thanks for coming. I couldn't go through this on my own.

SANDY: You did the test right?

VANESSA: First thing this morning. Like it said. What if it's positive? I'll kill myself, Sand! I will!

SANDY: Don't even talk like that. Where is it?

VANESSA: The test, you mean? In that drawer, behind my jumpers. Will you look to see what colour it is?

SANDY (*rising*): Right. May as well get it over with.

VANESSA: If it's pink, I'm all right. Please God, don't let it be . . . Please.

SANDY: What's that Steve say about this? After all, it's his fault.

VANESSA: I've not told him. I can't blame him. We're usually so careful.

(SANDY *opens drawer.*)

SANDY: Well, it only takes once.

VANESSA: The test, Sand? What colour?

SANDY: It's pink, Van. It's pink!

VANESSA: Let's have a look. (*Takes test*) Thank God. If I'd been pregnant I'd have killed myself, Sand.

SANDY: Forget that. Let's celebrate. Have a liquorice allsort! (*She gives* VANESSA *one from a bag, and eats the last herself*)

VANESSA: Ta. Here, I'd better get rid of this test.

SANDY: Put it in this paper bag.

VANESSA: If me mum found it I wouldn't have to kill myself. She'd do it for me.

SANDY: You can't go through this every month, Van. You'll have to go on the pill.

VANESSA: I was going to go to me doctor. But Helen Marshall, she went to him. He was a bit sticky.

SANDY: How d'you mean?

VANESSA: He tried to persuade her to talk it over with her mother. So she just walked out.

On the Pill

SANDY: Well, that was a bit silly.

VANESSA: I'd have done the same. Does your mum know, Sand, that you're sleeping with Pete, that you're on't pill?

SANDY: No. She's not as bad as your mum. But I don't know how she'd take it.

VANESSA: I think it's the fact that my father's dead, that she's on her own, that makes Mum like she is. She doesn't want me to have a life of my own, always prying into what I'm doing, what I'm thinking even —

SANDY: I'd not put up with that.

VANESSA: I just lie, tell her what she wants to hear. What else can I do?

SANDY: Look, Nessa, about the pill. Come to the clinic where I go. They're all right there.

VANESSA: I don't know —

SANDY: It's better than getting pregnant, than you thinking about killing yourself!

VANESSA: Yeah. I'll go. Will you come with me?

SANDY: I'll even make the appointment for you. Just be careful, though, your mum doesn't find the pills. I always keep mine on me.

VANESSA: Let's have a look.

SANDY: They're in me bag. (*She hands them over*) Here.

VANESSA: Amazing. Such a tiny pill can stop you getting pregnant.

(MRS CLAYTHORPE *enters*.)

MRS CLAYTHORPE: I thought I heard voices —

VANESSA (*horrified*): Mum!

MRS CLAYTHORPE: Auntie was poorly, so I came back early. Hullo, Sandra.

SANDY: Hullo, Mrs Claythorpe.

MRS CLAYTHORPE: Vanessa, what's the matter? What have you got behind your back?

VANESSA (*desperate*): Nothing, nothing, Mum.

MRS CLAYTHORPE: Don't be silly. Give it here, love. I'm waiting.

(VANESSA *hands over the pills*.)

SANDY: They're ... they're mine, Mrs Claythorpe.

MRS CLAYTHORPE: Pills! Drugs! I'll have the police on you, Sandra Barrett.

VANESSA (*protesting*): But Mum —

MRS CLAYTHORPE: Just a moment. These are contraceptive pills.

SANDY: I was just . . . showing them to Vanessa.

MRS CLAYTHORPE: I see. Showing off, were we?

(SANDY *and* VANESSA *are silent.*)

MRS CLAYTHORPE: Disgusting. On't pill. At your age. Your mother doesn't know what you're up to, I'll be bound.

SANDY: It's none of your business, Mrs Claythorpe.

MRS CLAYTHORPE: Cheeky with it. If I were your mother, you'd be out of the house in two minutes flat, I can tell you.

SANDY (*ignoring* MRS CLAYTHORPE): I'm going, Vanessa.

MRS CLAYTHORPE: Here, take these with you.

SANDY (*sarcastic*): Thank you, Mrs Claythorpe.

MRS CLAYTHORPE: And stay away from my daughter, you hear that.

SANDY (*ignoring* MRS CLAYTHORPE): Goodbye, Vanessa.

VANESSA (*tearful*): Bye, Sandra.

(SANDY *goes.*)

MRS CLAYTHORPE: A slut, that's what she's turned into.

VANESSA: Sandra's not like that, Mum.

MRS CLAYTHORPE: I know what's in store for her. Two kids before she's twenty and a husband — if she's lucky! I've seen it happen. Well, it's not happening to you!

VANESSA: It won't.

MRS CLAYTHORPE: You're going to college. That means passing exams. Not wasting time with that Steve.

VANESSA: Steve's all right.

MRS CLAYTHORPE: You're too young to be going steady. I shall tell him. You're not to see him any more.

VANESSA: But Mum . . . please, Mum —

MRS CLAYTHORPE: I know what's best for you, love. You'll thank me one day.

VANESSA (*with all her courage*): Mum, can't we talk about it?

MRS CLAYTHORPE: There's nothing to talk about. It's decided. (*Going*) I'll get your tea, and then go round to Mrs Barrett's.

On the Pill

VANESSA: You're not going to tell her, Mum, about Sandra?

MRS CLAYTHORPE: I've a duty. She has a right to know. We hear too much about children's rights these days. It's parents' rights we should be talking about.

VANESSA: But Mum – you can't go round there.

MRS CLAYTHORPE: I'd want to know if you were up to that sort of thing. Not that you ever would, I know that. Now come and have your tea ...

(*They go out.*)

SCENE 2 *The Barretts' sitting-room.*

MR *and* MRS BARRETT *enter, obviously upset.*

MR BARRETT: Well!

MRS BARRETT: I can't believe it! Sandra, on't pill. I'm her mother, and I'd no idea.

MR BARRETT: It's a shock. Aye, it's a shock, right enough.

MRS BARRETT: Stupid. But in a way, I wish Mrs Claythorpe hadn't told us.

MR BARRETT: It's that Pete, I suppose. She's out with him now.

MRS BARRETT: To think we've had him here in the house, made him welcome. While all the time behind our backs –

MR BARRETT: We should have thought. They've been going out together quite a time.

MRS BARRETT: Sandra. Seems only yesterday that she was ...

MR BARRETT: Had to happen some time.

MRS BARRETT: Not yet, Eddie. She's so young. We talked about it a few months ago. But she gave me no idea then that she was ... no idea at all.

(SANDY *enters. She wears outdoor clothes.*)

SANDY: It's raining cats and dogs.

MRS BARRETT: Sandra!

SANDY: Pete's popped into the off-licence. We thought we'd stop in. Hey, what's up?

MR BARRETT: Mrs Claythorpe's just been round here.

SANDY: Why, the old cow –

Family Frictions

MRS BARRETT (*very upset*): I thought I'd brought you up to know what's right. I'm sure I did my best.

MR BARRETT: We did trust you, love. You know that.

SANDY: How dare that woman come here! Interfering in my private business behind my back!

MRS BARRETT: Wouldn't matter, would it, if you'd nothing to hide?

SANDY (*defensive*): So . . . I'm on the pill. So what?

MRS BARRETT: It's not as simple as that. What it means . . . well, you know what it means.

SANDY: It's nowt to do with you, Mum.

MRS BARRETT: It's everything to do with us. You're our daughter, Sandra.

SANDY: It's my body. It's my life, Mum.

MRS BARRETT: You do happen to live in our house!

SANDY: I can't have sex in *your* house, is that it?

MRS BARRETT: No shame, Eddie. I can't believe it's Sandra talking.

MR BARRETT (*placating*): What your mother means, love – that it is our house, and while you live with us it's not unreasonable we should have a say in what goes on.

MRS BARRETT: How long have you been . . . since you were twelve, thirteen?

SANDY: If you're asking if I'm a nymphomaniac, just come straight out with it.

MR BARRETT: You're mother thinks no such thing.

MRS BARRETT: When you get a place of your own I shan't be responsible. You can carry on as you please.

SANDY: Like a tart, eh, Mum? Is that what you mean? It's the only work round here that pays.

MRS BARRETT: What a thing to say!

SANDY: Mum, I could be married now, I could have a kid, I'm old enough.

MRS BARRETT: That's different.

SANDY: Why?

MRS BARRETT: Then we'd have time, time to adjust to . . . I don't know.

MR BARRETT: You can imagine how we felt, it coming out of the blue, from that Mrs Claythorpe.

On the Pill

SANDY: I just don't get this. Why all the fuss? It's not as if the pill weren't around when you were my age. The swinging sixties! Everyone was on the pill!

MRS BARRETT: In London, maybe. But not up here. I wouldn't have dreamt. No one would . . .

SANDY: Then times have changed. Don't you realise that?

MRS BARRETT: If only you'd told me. Oh, Sandra, I thought we were so close.

SANDY: Look, I don't want to talk about it.

MRS BARRETT: Being so secretive. That's what hurts, Sandra.

PETE (*calls, off*): Hullo? It's me.

SANDY: That's Pete. I'm off.

MRS BARRETT: Oh, no you don't.

MR BARRETT: You stay right there. (*Going*) I'll fetch him here.

SANDY (*calls after him*): Dad . . . (*to* MRS BARRETT) If you say a word to Pete, I'll never forgive you.

PETE (*off*): What is it Mr Barrett?

MR BARRETT (*off*): In here. We want a word with you.

(PETE *and* MR BARRETT *enter.*)

PETE: Hi there, Sand. Mrs Barrett.

SANDY: Come on, Pete. We're going.

MR BARRETT: Just a moment.

SANDY: Don't listen, Pete. Take no notice.

PETE: Hang on. Is something wrong?

MRS BARRETT: Is something wrong?

MR BARRETT: We've found out that you and Sandra, well, I think you understand what I'm saying.

SANDY (*in tears*): You make it sound so sordid! You've no right.

MR BARRETT: Well, young man, what have you got to say for yourself?

PETE (*uneasy*): Yeah . . . well . . .

MRS BARRETT: We'd no idea. None. We thought you were a decent sort of lad.

PETE: Look, me and Sand, it's serious, you know. I'm not the sort of bloke who . . . well, just with anyone.

SANDY: You've no need to justify yourself to them –

PETE: I just want to set things straight. I wouldn't like them to think –

SANDY: Who cares what they think! They're trying to ruin our lives, that's all.

PETE: Come on, don't get in a state, eh?

SANDY: Have you had to go through this, this inquisition from your parents?

PETE: No. But, well, it's not the same, is it?

MRS BARRETT: No, with lads, you know, it's not the same.

MR BARRETT: You're more vulnerable, love. That's how it is.

SANDY: Not on the pill, I'm not going to get pregnant.

MR BARRETT: That pill, it's a health hazard. Specially for girls who start it young. Cancer, thrombosis —

SANDY: There's risks in everything. Sitting here, the ceiling could fall down.

PETE: It's true, Sand, about taking the pill. You know I wasn't keen on you taking it.

SANDY: They had a pill for men, but they didn't market it.

PETE: Aye, but you said you'd not trust the blokes to take it!

MRS BARRETT: Listen to them, Eddie. Quite the little man and woman of the world!

MR BARRETT: Well, at least they have talked things over, Ann.

MRS BARRETT: If Sandra had talked it over with us, that'd be more to the point.

SANDY: It's my decision. I'm seventeen. You just won't accept I'm grown up, will you? Perhaps it's because it makes you feel old. You want me to stay a child forever!

MRS BARRETT: Grown up! You don't even make your bed of a morning.

SANDY: What's that got to do with it?

MRS BARRETT: It shows you're not as grown up as you make out.

SANDY: Keeping your room tidy! That's a definition of being grown up, is it?

MR BARRETT: What your mother means is you're not responsible, not in the adult sense.

SANDY: I was responsible enough to go to the clinic. You ought to be glad I went, that I had the commonsense — and the nerve. It took nerve, you know, going along on me own. Or would you rather I got pregnant, and then had to have an abortion? Or an unwanted child?

On the Pill

MRS BARRETT: There is an alternative, love. It's called self-restraint. Sex isn't a thing to be taken lightly, you know.

SANDY: You think we don't know that.

PETE: Like I said, Mrs Barrett, with Sand and me, it's not something casual —

SANDY: What if it was? It's for *us* to decide, not them.

PETE: Look, they are your parents, Sand. I mean for them to be ... well, concerned, it's ... natural.

MRS BARRETT: You should be grateful we care enough, that we take the trouble.

MR BARRETT: Plenty of lasses aren't so lucky, Sandra.

MRS BARRETT: It'd be a lot easier for us, just to stand aside.

PETE: They do have a point, you know. I reckon if you were my daughter, I'd —

SANDY: What do you mean? If I were your daughter?

PETE: Well, I'd want to know what was going on.

SANDY: I don't believe this! You're on their side!

PETE: It's not a question of sides. I just, well, I can understand how they feel.

SANDY: Great! Then can you understand how I feel, having my fellow side with them against me? Leaving me, on me own, to fight for what's right for us? Some man you are! Tough on the outside, but a wimp underneath!

PETE (*just keeping cool*): All I said was I could see their point of view, that's all.

SANDY: Then you can see it on your own! Because I don't want to see you again! There, Mum, Dad, I hope you're satisfied! I'm through with him, sex, men, the pill, everything!

MRS BARRETT (*upset*): There's no need for that —

SANDY (*raging, in tears*): From now on I just ask you to keep out of my life! Just ... just keep out.

(SANDY *storms off.*)

MR BARRETT (*sighs*): Oh, heck!

PETE: I'd best go after her.

(*He goes out.*)

MRS BARRETT: Storming off like that, Eddie. It just shows, she's still a child, just a child.

Blackout.

Notes

How the plays came about

When we first met, the producer and the three writers, it was up to us what shape the plays would take. What did we want to say, what questions did we want to set up, and how were we to go about it? When you read these plays, remember that they are the result of a large number of small (but important) decisions. It was by choice that they came to be as they are. You would certainly have written them differently, and indeed we hope you may be inspired by these plays to write your own. The way we went about creating them may give you ideas of how to begin.

Developing the plays for this kind of performance meant that we had to agree on a setting, and on the same main group of characters. It would be through the eyes of these characters that the audience would be involved in five important issues of today.

The issues we chose were the kind that confront young people as they begin to take responsibility for their own lives, and so we invented Sandy and her boyfriend Pete. Because we wanted to avoid stereotypes, we decided that Sandy would be the more forceful of the two, and perhaps the more mature for her age. But both she and Pete share a lot of uncertainties; they have yet to explore and make up their minds on a whole range of issues that affect young people in the world today.

We also needed representatives of the adult world – characters who would put the point of view of authority and responsibility – and so Sandy's parents, Eddie and Ann came about. But, like all people, they would have their failings. They might fail to see that Sandy and Pete were old enough to have their own valid points of view. In taking on responsibilities, Ann and Eddie might have made all sorts of compromises with their lives that could seem wrong to Sandy and Pete.

It was clear from the start that not all the issues we wanted to deal with could be contained within these four characters. We would need other catalysts. And so grew the grandfather who puts demands on the family; the brother who, as a member of the armed forces, has made fighting a trade; the friend who is a pacifist; the friend who nearly gets pregnant. These, we hoped, would trigger off the dramatic situations.

As for the setting, ideally we needed a single place for each play, because there would be little chance of changing scene in the allotted fifteen minutes of performance. We also needed a place that could be both private and public. The café that we chose had these possibilities. It also enabled us to dramatise Eddie and Ann's means of income, and potentially give Sandy a job. We imagined a rather ordinary little café, the sort that you might find in Station Road, in a small northern city where jobs were few and far between.

The café didn't quite solve all our problems. In *Battle Lines* we needed a scene in a park; in *On the Pill* and *End of the Road* we moved away entirely, to the houses where the characters live. As you will find, *End of the Road* is the most private of all the plays. Choice of setting is in itself an important part of what a play says.

Using the plays

Small group readings followed by discussion will give an initial access to each play. Ideally the play should then either be developed into a polished reading, or be workshopped so that each group has a chance to act it. This is because a play really only comes to life when it is worked on in depth.

Some teachers will of course find that their aims can best be met by a single reading. They will want to get straight on to discussing the issues involved.

Workshopping

Acting a play does not necessarily mean acting to the rest of the class. Providing the teacher and those in nearby classrooms don't mind the noise level, small groups can act their plays at the same time in different corners of the room. One advantage of this method is that shy groups can gain confidence 'under cover'. There is also less likelihood of running out of time, so that all groups get a chance to act.

It is rare that a class conveniently divides into groups all of the right size. 'Spare' students can be assigned as an 'outside eye' to comment on the work of a group. It is important that they should not become theatre directors, because that will mean the 'actors' learn less; nor should they become fault-finding critics. Their job is simply to reflect back to the acting group what they see, what is good about it, what doesn't work, what doesn't make sense, what might need to be improved.

Workshopping, to be most effective, should go through a number of stages. These are some suggestions:

1　Each group casts the play and reads it through while sitting down.
2　Discussion. Did the casting seem right? What did they not understand in the dialogue. What seemed unclear in the action? The group should not expect to answer all questions at this stage.
3　Perhaps re-cast. Read it through again, still sitting down.
4　Discuss a setting. Where should the counter, table, chairs go? Where do entrances take place? Then create the setting with desks, chairs, etc.
5　Read the play through, putting in entrances, exits, some moves, and letting some of the emotions come through more strongly.

For many lessons, this will be as far as a group needs to go, particularly if the aim is to start writing or discussion on the issues raised by the play.

Some groups, particularly drama groups, may take the process some stages closer to performance:

6　Discuss and break down the play into sections or 'movements'. Give each a title, e.g. Sandy exposes Pete's so-called job; Pete explains why he's in the Platoon; Grandad's final disillusionment.
7　Rehearse these separate sections to make them illustrate their titles very clearly.

8   Discuss how the sections contrast in mood and tempo with each other. Run through the whole play trying to make these contrasts clear. (This is called 'pacing' the play.) Where does the climax occur?

9   Discuss how each character changes during the play. (Some, of course, may change very little.) Rehearse the whole play concentrating on making the character changes very clear.

10 Add simple costume and props and perhaps some lighting, and let each group give a workshop performance to the rest of the class.

A further extension to this kind of work is to write or improvise alternative endings to the plays.

All this work on the plays can be enriched by asking group members to compile dossiers of newspaper and magazine cuttings related to the theme of the play.

For groups who are not prepared to write essays, another way of developing critical writing is to design a theatre programme for a particular age-range (e.g. teenagers a year or two younger) with introductory notes on the play, and collages of material related to the subject matter.

Materials such as these, along with rehearsal and discussion notes, might well form the basis of a GCSE folder.

Suggestions for writing and discussion on each play

'Get a Job'

When the play was written, sixteen-year-old school-leavers could have the option of a one-year Youth Training Scheme. This has subsequently been extended to a two-year scheme. Many other countries have similar options for unemployed school-leavers.

Classes reading the play should amend any factual details about the YTS to bring it up to date. In other countries the name of the scheme should be changed to the local equivalent.

There are two main kinds of YTS in Britain at the time of publication. One is college-based and involves lectures and class work with supervised periods of training in local workplaces. The second is completely workplace based, but the employer is expected to arrange a schedule of training and to see that YTS members complete it. At the end of the YTS, each member gets documentation recording their achievements, and this is intended to be shown to prospective employers.

The main advantages of the scheme are that young schoolleavers who can't get a job have another option to going on social security. The YTS gives them experience of regular time-keeping and adapting to a workplace environment, as well as the specific skills related to the particular work experience. It should make them more attractive to prospective employees.

The disadvantages are that YTS schemes may not seem like 'real' work. They may appear to be (or may actually be) a way for employers to get a supply of cheap labour for menial tasks. They may also be a way of replacing expensive apprenticeships. Because the YTS is for a set period, no redundancy payments are involved. Because YTS trainees are not counted as unemployed, opponents have suggested that the schemes have a political value in reducing unemployment statistics.

Discussion

1 What makes Sandy storm off at the end of the play?
2 Is YTS a useful step – as Eddie thinks – to getting a proper job?
3 Is working in your parents' business good work experience, or are there drawbacks?
4 Is YTS a way for businesses to get cheap labour, while the government gets lower unemployment figures?
5 Does YTS avoid the need for apprenticeships?
6 How realistic is it to wait (as Sandra intends to) for the right job to turn up?
7 Is school worth it, especially the sixth form? Does striving for exams make sense nowadays?

Notes

8 How much of a threat is automation to different kinds of jobs? Compare the possibility of the 'café robot' with the robots that already exist in car assembly plants.
9 What steps can you take to create a job for yourself? (How do you think Eddie came to set up the café?)
10 Does 'someone' have a responsibility to create worthwhile jobs? And if so, who should the 'someone' be – a local industrialist, the local council, a co-operative, central government?

Writing

1 Imagine yourself as Sandy. At the end of the play you rush off to your bedroom and confide all your feelings to your diary. What do you write?
2 Imagine yourself as Pete. Eddie and Ann advise you to leave Sandy alone for the time being. You go home and decide to explain to Sandy in a letter why you think it's right for you to go on the YTS. What do you write?
3 As Sandy (or Pete), write to your best friend to explain how your feelings about Pete (or Sandy) have changed as a result of what's happened.
4 Write a comic short story to the title, 'The Robot Café'.
5 How important is work to the way we value ourselves? Write about the experiences of an ordinary person in a world where all work is carried out by robots.

Role-play and oral English

1 As Pete (or Sandy), recreate a telephone call to your best friend, in which you go over your reasons for (not) accepting YTS.
2 As Eddie and Ann discuss how to deal with Sandy. Decide which of you will go up to her bedroom. Role-play either Eddie or Ann dealing with Sandy.
3 Imagine a group of you were eavesdropping from a table in the café. Over another round of coffee or Coke, discuss your own opinions of Sandy's and Pete's points of view.
4 Talk to, or interview with a cassette-recorder, someone

who is on a YTS. Beforehand, work out the questions you will ask. Afterwards, prepare a summary and present it to the class, perhaps playing a few seconds of the recording as an illustration.

5   Debate, with chairman, proposer, opposer, and seconders, the good and bad points of YTS. You can think up your own motion, which might be along these lines: 'We believe that in the present situation, YTS offers the best hope for unemployed school-leavers.'

It will be even better if you can find a proposer and opposer who are committed in real life for and against YTS. The proposer might be a local YTS tutor, or a businessman or personnel officer. The opposer might be a local councillor or trade unionist. (Try your school governors.)

'Battle Lines'

Perhaps there's violence in all of us. The question is, can we control it, or does it get the better of us?

In 'Battle Lines' Sandy slowly comes to realise there's a lot about her boyfriend Pete that she didn't know to begin with. When he meets her, bruised and dishevelled, she thinks he's been on the receiving end of a fight. Only later does it emerge that he is a member of the Platoon, a group that enjoys organised hooliganism at football grounds. But because Platoon members wear smart clothes, and are well-disciplined, their appearance leads to them being acquitted in court of starting a fight.

Set against Pete and the Platoon is Sandy's brother Richard who is in the Navy and fought in the Falklands War. For Sandy there is no comparison, but Pete feels that he and Richard share feelings of pride and courage. For Pete there is no difference between being in a gang fight and being a member of the armed forces in combat. The play ends in a tense stalemate and invites resolution by the audience or reader.

Notes

Discussion

1   Why is Sandy so completely exasperated with Pete?
2   Is teenage violence (aggro) ever justified?
3   Why do some teenagers find aggro satisfying?
4   Are 'soft' parents to blame for teenage aggro, as Eddie thinks?
5   Do we all need to defend our little bit of territory? What means of defence do you think are acceptable?
6   Is joining the Territorials/Army/Navy/Air Force an acceptable way of channeling violent and aggressive feelings into a useful outlet?
7   Does society need such an outlet? And is that one of the values of the armed forces?
8   Should we bring back conscription?
9   Is violence different (for victim and for perpetrator) when it's carried out by long-range weapons instead of fists?
10 Do smartly dressed people stand a better chance of being let off by a magistrate?
11 Does the fear of prison deter teenagers from violence?

Writing

1   As Sandy, confide in your diary your feelings about Pete and the Platoon.
2   As Pete, write to Sandy, trying to heal the split. Can you justify the Platoon to Sandy, or should you renounce it for her sake?
3   As Sandy, or as yourself, write to a brother in the Navy. Either explain to him why you think he is justified in being part of a fighting arm of the country's defences, or explain why you think he should leave the Navy. In either case, draw parallels with Pete.
4   As a reporter, write a 500-word article on teenage violence. First, you might decide on the newspaper you work for, and vary your style accordingly.
5   As the same reporter, write up Pete's court case. What stance do you take when you come to assessing what's gone on?
6   Using Pete's case as an example, write a leader for the local

paper. (A leader is an expression of the newspaper editor's own viewpoint.)

7   Imagine yourself as a victim of an act of violence by football hooligans. Write, first of all, an angry letter of complaint to the local newspaper. Then, some time later, write a letter of forgiveness to your attacker.

8   Write two advertisements, one for the armed forces and one for peace.

9   As a magistrate, write a summary of your judgment in letting off Pete.

Role-play and oral English

1   Give a piece of your mind to a friend who has kept you waiting a long time.

2   Knowing that you're an hour late for an appointment, work out what you can say to win round the person you are meeting.

3   Talk to, and perhaps interview with a cassette-recorder, a member of the armed forces. Do the same with someone from your local peace movement. Try to find out why they feel as they do. Summarise their positions for presentation to the class, using one taped illustration for each.

4   Prepare and give a reasoned talk on whether a submariner (or aircraft pilot, or machine-gunner) is as responsible for dealing out death as someone who kills with a hand-held weapon.

5   Invent the court scene, basing it on Pete's description.

'End of the Road'

Sandy's grandad has been staying in her house while he recovers from an illness. Now that he is better, the family have to decide what's to be done with him. He may be unable to look after himself now. At the same time, Sandy's parents don't feel that he should be entrusted to an old people's home. When the grandad senses their unwillingness to keep him, he takes the matter into his own hands, leaving Sandy's mum in particular tormented with guilt.

Notes

Discussion

1 The grandfather is selfish. Should this affect any decision by the family?
2 Is Sandy too hard on her grandfather?
3 – or is she justified in sticking up for her own rights?
4 How much right do old people have to stay in their own home? Does this right change the more they become a burden on others?
5 Is an old person solely the responsibility of their family? How responsible should the state be?
6 Is there good enough provision for old people?
7 Can you truly accept that you too will be old one day?
8 Should voluntary euthanasia be available? If so, what safeguards might be needed? Would euthanasia cause relatives a moral dilemma?

Writing

1 Imagine one of your grandparents is staying in your home with no definite end to the visit in sight. Confide in your diary how you honestly feel.
2 Suppose one of your grandparents had been staying, and then left for the same reasons as Sandy's. Write a letter to your grandparent to explain how you feel about the situation.
3 Imagine yourself as Sandy's grandfather. (Imagine a grandmother in the same situation, if you prefer.) After returning home, you settle down to write to the family, explaining your reasons for leaving. Decide in advance whether the kind of person you are imagining would try to make them feel guilty or not.
4 Imagine you suddenly become unable to walk very steadily, and can only take a few steps at a time. You are kept in a special home which is pleasant and friendly, but you have little privacy amongst a lot of other people like you. All your friends seem to have been left outside. Choose one of them, and write to explain how you feel.
5 Write about your life now as you might remember it in the year 2040.

6 Write a story about a future society where no one is allowed to live beyond the age of thirty.

7 Visit an old people's home, and write a report on the quality of life for people living there. (You could base this on tape-recorded interviews.)

Role-play and oral English

1 Two of you discuss the (imaginary) failings of a third person who overhears. What happens?

2 Role-play a relative or a social worker persuading an old person to go into an old people's home.

3 An elderly relative is being kept alive by all the means available in a modern hospital. You receive a letter from the relative (dictated to a nurse) in which they say, 'I'd rather die than put up with the pain, the injections, and all the medicines. I'm sick and tired of being forced to stay alive when life has nothing more to offer me. Please tell the doctors to stop medication and allow it all to end.'

You call a family meeting to discuss the request. In groups, allocate different members of the family (young and old, close and distant relatives), and role-play the meeting. You could begin by reading out the letter.

4 Debate the proposition, 'Euthanasia should be available to all.'

'Stand Up and Be Counted'

Sandy hasn't thought much about pressure groups until an old school-friend, Carol, asks her to display a CND* poster. Her brother Richard, a naval rating, argues with Carol that pacifism is out of place in the sort of world we live in, and that armed forces are needed to keep the peace.

Sandy asks her dad about displaying the poster, but he is adamantly against it, arguing that such an open display of politics would lose him customers.

On reflection, Sandy admires Carol's stand. She begins to realise that perhaps it's important that there are people who are prepared to 'stand up and be counted'. If the poster can't go up in the café, at least she can put it up in her bedroom window.

*CND: Campaign for Nuclear Disarmament.

Notes

Discussion

There are really two discussions which can follow on from this play. You can discuss the issue of pacifism versus armed struggle, and whether nuclear weapons alter the argument substantially. Alternatively, you can discuss the general point about the need for people to make a stand on something they feel strongly about. Of course, many discussions will contain both elements but the teacher or chairperson should be aware of the two possibilities.

1 Is it fair to put people on the spot, as Carol does the Barrett family with the poster?
2 Don't we all have a responsibility at least to consider important issues?
3 Can ordinary individuals have any effect on wider events?
4 Are people who canvass on doorsteps and go on demonstrations misguided?
5 Is it sufficient to give money to a cause you believe in (Trade unions, political parties, CND, anti-apartheid movement)?
6 Would you be put off going to a café or shop (or dealing with any other kind of business) if they openly showed support for a particular cause? How much does it depend on whether or not you agree with the particular cause?
7 Is it possible to be neutral? For example, does Eddie's refusal to put up the poster in fact support the argument for the armed forces? Is silence tacit support for the majority view?

Writing

1 Recall an event in your own life when you have made a stand on some issue. It might have been on the way you dress, or personal habits like smoking, or moral dilemmas like reporting someone who has done wrong. It might be making a stand on a matter of conscience, or a religious matter.

Write up the event as though for your own diary. Also write the event through the eyes of either someone you were making the stand against, or of someone on the sidelines.

2   Write a letter to a friend who you know will disagree, explaining why you have taken a stand on some particular issue.

3   Imagine an older person who has gone to prison for their beliefs. Write them a letter of sympathy and encouragement. You might then rewrite your letter in the knowledge that it will be censored by the prison authorities before it reaches the person you are writing to.

4   Write a persuasive advertisement for CND to go in an armed forces magazine, and an advertisement for one of the armed forces to go in *Sanity*, the CND journal. Alternatively, choose any group, and write a persuasive advertisement to go in a magazine of opposing viewpoint (e.g. an advertisement for Sizewell Pressurised Water Reactor in the Friends of the Earth magazine, and an anti-Sizewell advertisement in *Power News*, the Central Electricity Generating Board journal).

5   Research and write up the life of an ordinary person who has come to have a strong influence on wider events (e.g. a member of CND, of a national resistance movement, of a trade union, of a minority religion). Alternatively, interview someone locally who is strongly committed to a cause, even though they may have found no fame (or notoriety). Write a piece about them for a local newspaper, and perhaps try to get it published.

Role-play and oral English

1   In pairs, imagine yourselves as Carol and Richard, and role-play their confrontation as they argue the merits of pacifism versus armed force.

2   Suppose Sandy had put up the poster in the café – or a similar one on some other hotly contested issue. Imagine yourselves as Sandy and an irate customer. Perhaps a third person might be a neutral bystander, and a fourth could be in favour of the poster.

3   Debate the proposal: 'Pacifism is a stab in the back for the armed forces.'

'On the Pill'

On the face of it, Sandy and Vanessa have very different parents, but when it comes to their sexual relationships the two mothers have much in common. Eddie still believes that standards of behaviour are different for boys.

Discussion

1 How much should you tell your parents about your relationships?
2 How much should they expect to know? Do parents have a right to know if you get contraception for yourself?
3 How much do these matters depend on age?
4 If there was a pill for men (health risks being equal) who in a relationship should be responsible for contraception?
5 Is there an argument in favour of sexual abstinence before marriage, even if your religious views don't require this?
6 Do you have a right to enjoy sexual relationships in the home you share with your parents?
7 When can sexual relationships make you 'cheap'?

Writing

1 You're afraid that a boyfriend or girlfriend is growing cool because your parents prevent you from having an opportunity to show your feelings. Write a letter to the friend explaining the situation.
2 A good friend tells you she is pregnant. (Alternatively, a good friend tells you he has got a girlfriend pregnant.) Write in your diary your views and feelings.
3 What do you think about abortions? Write a letter explaining your views to someone who holds the opposite view.
4 There has been a debate about abortion in the local paper. Write a letter for publication putting your point of view as strongly as possible.
5 Find out about, and write a group report on, the different forms of contraception, their good points and drawbacks. (Your Family Planning Association will have leaflets and information.)

Family Frictions

Role-play and oral English

1   Role-play what would happen in your family if you were in a relationship like Sandy and Pete.
2   A good friend tells you she is pregnant. Alternatively, a good friend tells you he has got a girlfriend pregnant. Role-play how you would counsel your friend.
3   Role-play parents with different attitudes to contraception having a discussion one evening when their teenage children are out.
4   Role-play a boyfriend telling his girlfriend she is 'cheap' because she has slept with someone before him. She knows (because he has told her) that he has done the same thing.

Note

The legal position on sexual relationships in Britain in 1987 is this:

A girl under the age of sixteen who has sexual intercourse does not herself break the law.

It is against the law for a male over fourteen to have sexual intercourse with a girl under thirteen. It is also against the law for a male to have sexual intercourse with a girl who is thirteen or over, and under sixteen, but there is an exception in this case. This is when the male is under twenty-four and believes, with good reason, that the girl is sixteen or over. He must not have been charged with this offence before.

So far as contraception advice is concerned, the legal position in Britain in 1987 is this (it is the result of a controversial case brought by Mrs Gillick which resulted in a House of Lords ruling):

A girl under sixteen may ask her doctor for contraceptive advice and get contraceptive prescriptions without her parents' consent, provided she has sufficient understanding and intelligence to know what she is doing.

The Lords did add, however, that normally medical treatment of a child under sixteen would be carried out with parental consent. The doctor should be trusted to judge what was in the best interests of the girl as his patient, and the doctor should persuade her to tell her parents, or to let the doctor do so.